THE LIKABILITY BLUEPRINT

THE LIKABILITY BLUEPRINT

Effortless Strategies to Boost Your Charisma

INNER POWER

Inner Strength Counselling

CONTENTS

1 INTRODUCTION 1
2 BE IMPRESSIVE 3
3 BE CONFIDENT AND ADAPTIVE 9
4 BE CHARISMATIC AND ATTRACTIVE 15
5 BE LIKED 21
6 COMMUNICATION AND RAPPORT BUILDING 27
7 PRESENTATION 31

CHAPTER 1

INTRODUCTION

Mastering the art of projecting a distinct persona, communicating effectively, and adapting responses can significantly broaden the spectrum of opportunities in your life. It holds the power to enhance personal relationships, foster attraction, and bolster success in sales.
By refining your presentation and cultivating an innate charm, you'll naturally garner more esteem from both friends and family. This transformation can also elevate your leadership qualities, making you more adept in any situation requiring interaction with others. Essentially, proficiency in communicating shapes every interaction positively.
This book aims not just to amplify your charisma and impressiveness but also to refine your persuasiveness, sales acumen, and efficacy in debates or discussions. With these tools at your disposal, you'll wield an influential presence, paving the way for success in various

spheres. Are you prepared to embark on this journey?

CHAPTER 2

BE IMPRESSIVE

Being likable and attractive can be tricky since these qualities differ from person to person. Instead, let's focus on something more concrete and repeatable: being impressive.

So, how do you ensure that after spending time with you, people walk away seeing you as someone remarkable and capable? This matters because when others find you impressive, they're more likely to value your opinions, want to collaborate, and take you seriously in general.

IMPRESSIVE RULES

Before we proceed further, let's discuss a crucial principle when it comes to impressing others: the cardinal rule is not to overtly try to impress them, or at the very least, not to make it obvious that you are trying.

Here's the rationale: when you visibly attempt to impress someone, it signals that you seek their validation. Consequently, it implies a hierarchy where they hold a higher status. If you're striving to impress them, it suggests you perceive them as more significant or impressive than yourself. Consequently, they might adopt the same belief.

Additionally, actively trying to impress creates an underlying agenda in your words and actions. It raises doubts about the authenticity of everything you say. For instance, are you genuinely passionate about poetry, or are you simply accentuating this interest to cater to their expectations?

At its worst, striving to impress can project a lack of self-awareness. The belief that you can easily deceive someone into being impressed without them recognizing your intentions often highlights a lack of understanding of how you're perceived.

Hence, this is the fundamental rule: to be more impressive, exude indifference, and remain authentic. Avoid overtly boasting or deliberately inserting your accomplishments into conversations. By projecting an attitude of not desperately seeking to impress, you convey that you don't require their validation, which is inherently more impressive and appealing.

KNOW YOUR STUFF

If you can't directly show your best qualities while talking, how can you still leave a good impression?

The most important thing is to know a lot about different things and speak confidently about them. How? By simply knowing your stuff.

Have you ever spoken to someone who knows a ton about something they're really interested in? It's hard not to be impressed after talking to them.

Most of us aren't experts in everything. We all have things we're passionate about and know a lot about. When you get the chance, talk about these things you love. This way, you'll talk with excitement and show what you know in a way that makes sense.

This book will keep talking about how passion can make you more interesting and impressive.

If you know you'll be talking about things you're not an expert in, do some research beforehand. For instance, if you're going to an industry conference, read up on that industry, the people attending, and the recent news.

ONE SIMPLE TRICK

Preparing before important meetings is smart, but what if you're not attending a specific event or if the conversation takes an unexpected turn?

The good news is there are some simple and effective strategies—these are the "easy wins." These involve learning and researching certain topics that can assist you in any conversation. For instance, staying updated on current news can make you seem knowledgeable and engaged in various situations. Similarly, if you're going to a new area or country, spending time learning about the place and recent events there can be really helpful.

OFFER MORE

The easiest way to seem impressive is to genuinely be impressive. If you have diverse interests, talents, and experiences, it's likely to show naturally.

Everyone should aim to develop themselves and broaden their skills, knowledge, and what they can offer. You don't have to specialize in just one thing; thanks to the internet, it's easy to become a multi-talented expert in various fields by learning online.

To speak impressively, find a subject you're passionate about. Your passion will reflect in your engaging and well-informed conversation. Choosing a field you love is crucial to being truly impressive.

There are other areas to develop besides expertise. Traveling, for example, broadens your understanding of the world and adds color to your experiences. Developing knowledge in health, psychology, literature, food, wine, art, film, and music also enriches your overall personality.

Expand your interests genuinely; don't force yourself to like something. And don't try too hard to impress. Instead, let your experiences and knowledge naturally color your conversations.

Listening is just as vital as speaking. Listening attentively without rushing to respond shows depth and intelligence. Every interaction is an opportunity to learn and grow.

Active listening involves repeating what you've heard to show understanding. This simple act demonstrates attentiveness and can make a big difference, even shown to increase tips for waiters who repeat orders.

ACTION SPEAKS LOUDER

To be more impressive, take action instead of just talking. It's a mistake to outright tell someone how impressive you are because when you talk too much about what you can do, people might think it's just empty talk.

Instead, demonstrate your abilities through action. Taking initiative without boasting beforehand suggests you're self-driven, proactive, and willing to take charge.

For instance, rather than talking about the amazing trips you plan to take, just go ahead and embark on those journeys. Similarly, instead of promising to lose weight, take action and work on it. Don't make commitments to be kind or helpful if you don't intend to follow through.

Let your actions speak louder than your words. For example, I once gained an incredible opportunity because, over two years, I consistently submitted my work on time. This reliability and follow-through built trust, and it's crucial not to break promises as it can damage your reputation.

In essence, show through your actions rather than merely talking about what you can or will do.

CHAPTER 3

BE CONFIDENT AND ADAPTIVE

To impress others and become more likable, developing confidence and adaptability is crucial. It's about being the kind of person who can smoothly adjust to any situation they're dropped into.

Imagine someone checking your LinkedIn profile and inviting you to their startup's office in another country for meetings and socializing. Sounds unusual, right? But it happened to me, and in today's world, such scenarios are increasingly likely to happen to you too. You may find yourself in a situation where you're meeting new people, conducting business, experiencing a different culture, and spending an entire night socializing with them.

If you're shy or awkward in such situations, it won't go smoothly. To make a positive impression, you must be at ease, confident, and approachable. Being outgoing and applying the strategies we've discussed earlier is essential in these scenarios.

These experiences provide networking opportunities crucial for achieving our goals. So, does this mean that natural introverts can't succeed? Not at all! It means they need to learn how to adjust their behavior to adapt to different social situations.

ANTI-SOCIAL-ANXIETY

When I was in high school, I wasn't always confident in social situations. As a natural introvert, I used to worry too much about what others thought. With practice and self-discipline, I managed to change this.

Similar to not trying too hard to impress others, it's crucial not to be overly concerned about what people think of you in a broader sense. Worrying about others' opinions can make you less authentic and relaxed. Overthinking might lead to second-guessing your actions and words, causing you to be too self-conscious.

Understanding that not everyone will like you is important. Accepting this fact without feeling bothered is key. In most cases, you won't need to interact with these people again, so their opinions shouldn't affect you significantly.

However, knowing this intellectually and feeling this way while interacting are different things. That's where practice and exposure play vital roles.

To overcome my inhibitions, I used to attend parties where I knew few people and practiced talking to new individuals. Exploring social situations with a friend and engaging with strangers helped me gain confidence and care less about others' opinions. This confidence became crucial in my career and personal life later on.

You can further enhance your confidence by using techniques from cognitive-behavioral therapy (CBT). Challenge unhelpful thoughts by testing them, like reminding yourself that most people are polite and wondering why it would matter if you were laughed at. Additionally, hypothesis testing involves deliberately saying or doing something you fear, like intentionally stuttering, to realize that the outcome isn't as bad as imagined.

Expose yourself to diverse situations; you'll learn that occasional awkwardness is fine. With time, you become desensitized to these situations, and they no longer intimidate you.

Moving beyond nerves and anxiety leads to calm confidence, making you socially resilient. To develop confidence and charisma faster, consider activities that break inhibitions, like stand-up comedy, acting, or martial arts.

These experiences help you grow and become more comfortable in various situations, ultimately leading to a more confident and socially adept you.

VARIETY

Having a friend from outside my school was immensely beneficial for me. It provided me with a more diverse group of friends, alleviating the pressure to impress a single social circle. I had multiple friend groups, which not only relieved the pressure but also exposed me to various personalities and perspectives.

Interacting with different people helped me become adaptable. This adaptability allowed me to become a social chameleon, capable of impressing everyone from my partner's parents to people with contrasting backgrounds, like football enthusiasts.

The trick is to stay true to yourself while adjusting your communication style and aspects of your personality as needed. Avoid acting out of character, as it can come across as insincere. Instead, choose what parts of yourself to display in different situations. For instance, restrain yourself from using offensive language when meeting your partner's parents while still showcasing your genuine humor. This shows respect and consideration.

Moreover, refrain from judging others based on their differences. Passing judgment can lead to reciprocated judgment, which doesn't bode well for relationships.

While you can learn these principles theoretically, nothing beats the practical experience gained from meeting various people and spending time with different personalities. Seize opportunities to expand your social circle and step out of your comfort zone. With time and exposure to diverse individuals, you might develop a sort of 'template' for interacting with different character types that you'll encounter in the future.

BE RELAXED AND CALM

Handling new situations or unexpected challenges with composure and control is a valuable skill. This ability often stems from cognitive-behavioral techniques (CBT), such as evaluating whether panicking in a situation truly helps or considering the worst possible outcome.

Understanding your body's response in high-pressure situations is crucial. Stress hormones like dopamine, norepinephrine, and cortisol trigger physical changes, preparing for confrontation. However, in situations where charm and wit are required, a racing mind can hinder performance.

Practicing desensitization can assist, but controlling your breath by inhaling and exhaling deeply activates the "rest and digest" state, countering fight-or-flight symptoms, and promoting calmness, and relaxation.

Conscious body language also influences your mental state. Adopting a relaxed posture can positively impact your mindset.

Being physically fit enhances confidence and the ability to handle adverse situations. Feeling capable physically reduces concerns about others' opinions or potential confrontations.

When things unexpectedly go wrong, maintaining calmness is crucial. Emotionally detaching yourself prevents impulsive actions and errors. Take a step back, assess the situation as an impartial observer, and consider the best steps for a favorable outcome. Implement CBT techniques to remind yourself of the ineffectiveness of panic and proceed methodically toward a solution.

CHAPTER 4

BE CHARISMATIC AND ATTRACTIVE

Attractiveness encompasses various aspects beyond mere physical appeal; it extends to being more appealing to the opposite sex and possessing magnetic, compelling traits that draw others to you. It's about being someone others want as friend, colleagues, or allies—someone who exudes confidence and charisma.

This concept of attractiveness traces back to our evolutionary past, where emotions and social behavior evolved to ensure survival within communities. People are naturally drawn to those they perceive as having the ability to support survival or aid in passing on their genetic legacy.

In the realm of dating and social interactions, humans seek individuals they believe hold a higher social 'rank,' as associating with such people elevates their own status and access to resources.

Much of human behavior is driven by the subconscious need to gain status, fit in, and demonstrate superiority within the societal hierarchy, all linked to the survival and propagation of our DNA.

Everyday actions, like wearing makeup or investing in lavish possessions, often subconsciously aim at signaling fertility or resources, thus enhancing one's desirability or perceived status among peers.

When interacting socially, trying too hard to impress or displaying nervousness can be counterproductive. Confidence and authenticity are key. Confidence communicates a lack of concern about others' opinions, often leading others to perceive you as being of similar or higher status.

This principle holds significance in dating as well. Attempting to impress someone instantly communicates a lack of self-worth, rendering oneself less attractive in their eyes.

In essence, being attractive extends beyond physical appearance and involves projecting confidence, authenticity, and a sense of belonging—traits deeply rooted in our evolutionary instincts.

HOW TO APPROACH PEOPLE

The concept of pickup artist techniques revolves around tactics designed to position oneself higher in the social hierarchy than the person they're interacting with. One such technique is the 'neg,' a backhanded compliment aimed at subtly undermining someone's confidence. For instance, approaching an attractive person and saying, 'You look amazing, even in that outfit!' The boldness of the statement may make the other person feel slightly less confident, prompting them to want to impress you in return.

While this approach might yield results for some, it's often considered cynical and unkind in the realm of dating. The importance of likability cannot be overstated, and people generally do not enjoy the company of individuals who make them feel bad. Moreover, if the person detects these tactics, it can backfire, making the initiator seem sleazy, mean-spirited, and unattractive.

An alternative approach involves sending signals of confidence while also being likable. Start by gauging the interest of the person you want to talk to—smile and observe their response. Engage not only with them but also with their group of friends (if they're present), spending nearly equal time with everyone. This portrays you as confident, outgoing, enjoyable, and not solely focused on one person. It creates an impression that you're sociable and may even prompt a sense of competition among your friends.

If the interaction progresses positively, find an opportunity to have a one-on-one conversation by inviting the person for a drink away from the group. By being sociable and confident with their friends and not overly fixated on one individual, they become more attractive and appealing to the person of interest.

CHARISMA

Charisma is a quality that's challenging to define precisely. When someone possesses charisma, they exude magnetism, leaving a lasting impression that makes us instantly want to connect with them. These individuals often exhibit natural leadership qualities and have the ability to captivate our attention effortlessly. Many celebrities like Dwayne "The Rock" Johnson, Michelle Obama, Oprah Winfrey, and Will Smith are prime examples of individuals with extraordinary charisma, drawing us in with their presence.

The root of charisma often lies in passion and authenticity—how congruent their words are with their actions. Charismatic people express themselves using their entire body, and their faces convey animated expressions. Research suggests that individuals who gesticulate more while communicating tend to be rated as more charismatic by observers. Gesturing with the body amplifies the message's credibility, indicating genuine belief in what's being said. This underscores the significance of body language in communication.

Should you attempt to force more gestures? While being mindful of your hand movements can be beneficial, genuine passion and belief in what you're expressing are paramount. Authenticity outweighs any attempts at feigned enthusiasm.

Expressing emotions is another crucial aspect of charisma, particularly evident in storytelling. Observing individuals like Will Smith narrate a story in an interview reveals their usage of vivid emotions, deliberate pauses, impersonations, and scene-setting. This storytelling style demands confidence as it involves the risk of building up a story significantly only to falter at the punchline. However, it fosters a deeper emotional connection as listeners can vicariously experience the emotions the storyteller felt. Gestures and facial expressions aid in this connection through the activation of "mirror neurons," which resonate with the emotions conveyed by others.

Practicing storytelling that engages the entire body and vividly illustrates scenes to the audience enhances charisma. Embrace the narrative without rushing to its conclusion, expressing genuine emotions. This approach makes you more compelling, relatable, and ultimately, more charismatic.

PERSUASION

Persuasion and charisma share a strong connection, enhanced by an understanding of others and the people you are engaging with. It's essential to recognize that human decision-making isn't solely driven by logic. We don't make choices purely because they're logically sound. Instead, our decisions are largely guided by emotional impulses.

Charisma and persuasion intersect here. They involve conveying emotions and ensuring that others comprehend the essence of your message. To achieve this, it's crucial to establish a value proposition—an emotional hook. In the context of selling, this means you're not just selling a product; you're selling a dream or a vision.

For instance:
- Instead of selling a games console, you're selling an experience of futuristic technology that enables thrilling adventures and exploration.
- Rather than merely selling a car, you're promoting status, comfort, safety, and freedom.

Similarly, in politics:
- You're not just promoting a political party; you're advocating for a vision of a better world.

When you can tap into the emotions underlying your message and align them with the desires and aspirations of the person you're addressing, you can influence their behavior effectively. Understanding how to connect emotionally with others and tailor your message accordingly becomes a potent tool for persuasion.

CHAPTER 5

BE LIKED

Derren Brown, a psychological illusionist, expresses discontent with books like "How to Make Friends and Influence People," arguing that being genuinely nice and likeable is a straightforward way to achieve both. According to Brown, doing nice things for people naturally fosters likability without needing any magic formula.

Often, we've overcomplicated the art of being likeable. For instance, in the section about meeting people at bars, engaging with others' friends reflects being enjoyable, less singularly focused, and considerate, traits that people generally appreciate.

There's a common misconception that "nice guys finish last" or that excessive niceness can be unattractive. However, the issue isn't about being nice but rather the motives behind it. Consider the stereotypical "nice guy" who is infatuated with a popular girl but doesn't express his true feelings. He lavishes her with gifts, compliments her excessively, yet she chooses to date seemingly "jerky" individuals instead.

The crux here isn't niceness but the lack of authenticity and confidence. These "nice guys" are not truly being nice—they're acting nice because they want something from the other person. This contrasts with the honesty of the so-called "jerks." In reality, most women desire someone kind but also seek confidence, coolness, and success. Imagine someone embodying all those qualities alongside genuine kindness!

Similarly, women who exhibit confidence and positive attention while being genuinely nice often attract men. This principle extends to career success as well. While there's evidence suggesting that some highly successful individuals in business may possess psychopathic traits, there are numerous prosperous individuals who are genuinely nice and decent. In many cases, being genuinely pleasant offers a significant advantage because people prefer working with individuals they enjoy spending time with.

MAKE PEOPLE LIKE YOU

SMILE

Smiling more often is really important. It's actually one of the most valuable things you can take away from this book!

Have you noticed how smiles can be contagious? That's because when we see someone smiling, it's hard not to smile back. Smiling also triggers something cool in our brains called facial feedback. It means that the expression on our face can affect how we feel. So, when we smile, we actually start feeling happier.

Here's the best part: when you smile and seem happy, it rubs off on others. They start feeling happier around you too. This makes them enjoy your company more and see you in a positive light. Not only that, but it shows people that you're enjoying yourself, and who doesn't love being around someone who's having a good time?

HAVE A GOOD TIME

Here's a tip: try to stay positive and have a good time wherever you are. People who genuinely enjoy themselves, even in serious situations, are really appealing. It might seem a bit simpleminded sometimes, but it's actually a great skill to have.

When you're having a good time, it shows that you can handle any situation well. Plus, it helps others feel more at ease and have a good time too. Even if you're in a serious meeting, finding some enjoyment in it can make a difference. And if you love what you do, enjoying your work makes everything better!

BE POSITIVE

Connecting with the previous point, staying positive is key. It's one of the best ways to make people like you and enjoy being with you.

Nobody wants to be around someone who's always negative and focuses on the negative things. But if you can see the good in situations, it makes the moments better instead of worse.

DO NOT GOSSIP

In a work environment, it's wise to avoid getting involved in office gossip or politics. Speaking negatively about colleagues or spreading rumors can cause harm not only to the people involved but also to your reputation. Others may question if you'd gossip about them in the same way or spread rumors about their actions.

REMEMBER THEIR NAMES

A small yet effective habit is to make an effort to remember people's names. This demonstrates your interest and can earn you some positive recognition from others. If remembering names is challenging for you, consider using mnemonic techniques. Try associating the name with sounds, recalling someone else you know with the same name, or linking it to a fictional character or celebrity you're familiar with.

ENCOURAGE OTHERS

One of the most impactful ways to enhance your likability is by uplifting others. Encouraging people, offering compliments, and acknowledging their accomplishments are powerful gestures. Complimenting someone not only boosts their confidence but also reflects positively on your own confidence. While putting others down might temporarily elevate your status, genuinely acknowledging someone's achievements showcases your confidence and your ability to recognize excellence.

There are subtle yet effective methods to support others. Take a moment to notice if someone in a group seems excluded or hesitant to join the conversation. Extend a hand and engage them in a conversation; this gesture won't go unnoticed. Additionally, encourage others to share by inviting them to contribute or take the lead in discussions. These actions can greatly contribute to creating a positive and inclusive environment.

LET THEM ELABORATE

A surefire way to hinder your likability is by making conversations solely about yourself. It's crucial to remember to engage others by asking about their thoughts and experiences, actively listening, and giving them the space to share what's on their mind. Being genuinely interested in others fosters a stronger connection and makes interactions more meaningful.

MANNERS

Good manners hold significant importance. They signify not only a well-rounded upbringing but also offer an opportunity to express gratitude and respect. What's remarkable about manners is their ability to bridge gaps. For instance, holding a door open for someone, even if you're their superior, demonstrates mutual respect regardless of the differences in job positions. Simple gestures like saying "please" and "thank you" are effortless yet powerful ways to express appreciation and showcase respect towards others.

CHAPTER 6

COMMUNICATION AND RAPPORT BUILDING

When meeting someone new, starting a conversation might feel challenging. The typical approach of asking about someone's job or favorite band often doesn't lead to a flowing chat. Even with friends, the common "what's new?" might not spark much. These questions often don't pave the way for engaging conversations; they're details easily found on social media.

A better icebreaker? How about asking, "How was your day?" It's a classic and immediately makes the conversation relevant and relaxed. Moreover, it often opens up the chance for more details that can be further explored. If their day was rough, why was that? Maybe they're not enjoying work—how long has that been going on?

The key to sustaining a conversation is to genuinely listen to what the other person says and then seize the opportunities to dive deeper and keep the chat flowing.

ALL CONVERSATIONS COUNT

It's essential not only to engage in conversation with those you want to impress but also with everyone in your life. When interacting with people like taxi drivers or waiters, you might not have time for lengthy talks, but a simple inquiry about their day or how they're doing can be nice. You never know who you might meet or what impression you might leave.

For those working in customer-facing roles, making conversation, offering well-wishes, and wearing a smile are crucial. Have you ever been served by someone who didn't even glance up? It's an unpleasant feeling and doesn't leave a favorable impression. Even if someone dislikes their job, disregarding these opportunities can hinder their progress, potential references, and personal growth. Regardless of job satisfaction, putting effort into your work and treating others well is always beneficial.

BUILD THAT RAPPORT

To establish a quick rapport or friendship, the usual advice involves mirroring body language and using similar language. However, this approach might feel insincere and doesn't foster genuine connections. A more effective way is to engage in deeper conversations. For instance, ask about personal aspects like how they handle frequent travel or their career aspirations. Sharing your own vulnerabilities can also balance the conversation and build trust.

Another strategy is to create shared experiences. It could be as grand as a night out or a trip, but even smaller activities, like trying a new drink together or teaming up for a harmless prank, can create shared moments that strengthen your bond as a team. These shared experiences contribute significantly to building a connection.

COMMUNICATION ART

Effective communication is a vital tool in various aspects of life, including business, relationships, and social interactions. It allows you to express your thoughts, emotions, and intentions, making understanding possible. Without strong communication skills, even the best strategies or intentions can fail.

The primary objective of communication is to convey a message in the most direct and efficient manner. It's not about using elaborate language or showcasing an extensive vocabulary. Instead, it's about delivering a message clearly and succinctly. However, a rich vocabulary allows you to express ideas more precisely with fewer words, offering subtle nuances and varied tones. This flexibility in language helps tailor your message to different audiences and situations, enabling better connections and understanding.

CHAPTER 7

PRESENTATION

The concept of physical attraction is not solely tied to women and their makeup or clothing choices. Men also exude attractiveness through youthful looks, a healthy physique displaying vitality and strength, and indicators of overall well-being like bright eyes, good skin, and healthy teeth. Symmetry in appearance is often associated with good health, while its absence might signal potential health issues.

Improving health is a potent method to enhance attractiveness. This involves regular exercise to ensure a toned body, adequate sleep, a balanced diet, stress management, and spending time outdoors. Neglecting health can hinder success and overall well-being.

Confidence also plays a pivotal role in attractiveness. Shyness or reluctance to wear clothes that showcase one's features may impede confidence. Confidence is highly appealing and attractive to both men and women. Acting and feeling confident is as crucial as physical appearance in being perceived as attractive.

For instance, a woman interested in a colleague might consider wearing clothes that exude confidence, such as a pencil skirt, high heels, and a smart hairstyle. It's not about solely appealing to someone else but about displaying self-confidence, which is incredibly attractive.

Similarly, for men, wearing a well-fitted suit or stylish accessories can exude confidence and success. Your attire isn't just about your appearance; it's about showing confidence, being aware of trends, and expressing yourself. Taking care of your appearance communicates self-worth and capability, traits that command respect.

Ultimately, projecting the right impression through your appearance is crucial, especially in professional settings where appearance often aligns with perceived capability and responsibility. It's about valuing oneself, and when you do, others are more likely to do the same.

www.ingramcontent.com/pod-product-compliance
Lightning Source LLC
Chambersburg PA
CBHW071325080526
44587CB00018B/3347